I'm Reading About

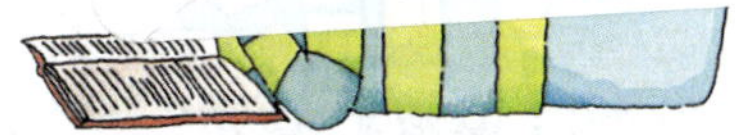

NEW HAMPSHIRE

The Granite State!

GALLOPADE

by Carole Marsh

Printed and Manufactured in Peachtree City, GA., USA
www.gallopade.com

Book design: John Hanson

Editorial manager: Janice Baker

New Hampshire is a great state.

It is one of a kind.

What makes New Hampshire special?

Let's read about it and see!

NATIVE AMERICANS

Who lived in New Hampshire first?

Native Americans did!

They moved around to find food.
They hunted in New Hampshire's woods.
They fished in New Hampshire's rivers.
They gathered fruits and seeds and nuts.

EXPLORERS

The first explorers came to New Hampshire in 1603.
They came from the country of England.

Martin Pring was their leader.
He and his men were looking for new land!

SETTLEMENT

The first settlement in New Hampshire was started by a group of fishermen. They called the settlement Pannaway Plantation. It was located at Odiorne Point. That's in the town of Rye today!

New Hampshire was one of the original 13 colonies.

Odiorne Point

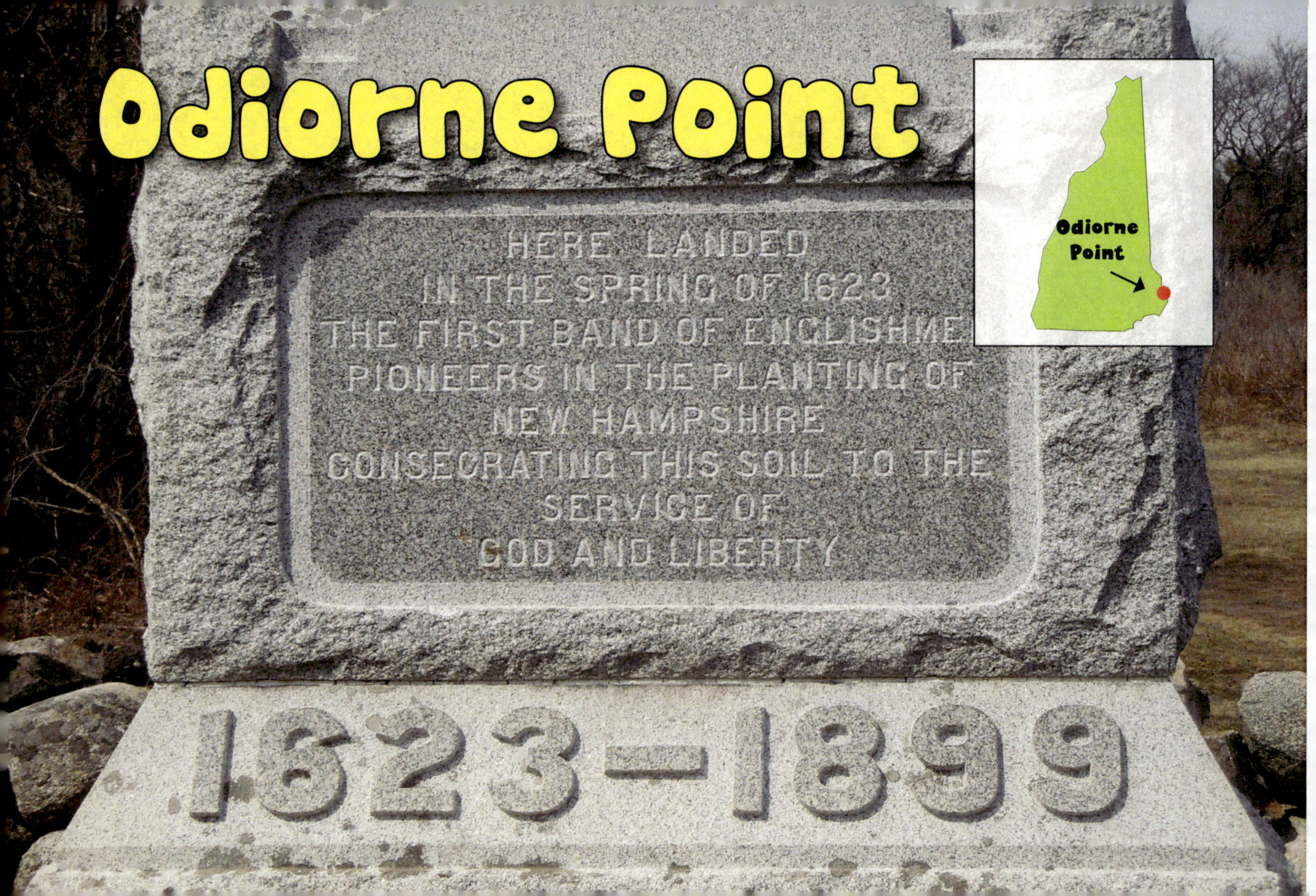

STATEHOOD

New Hampshire was the ninth state
to join the United States of America!

Isn't it great,
to be a state!
I bet New Hampshire
could hardly wait!

New Hampshire became a state in 1788.

New Hampshire
The 9th State

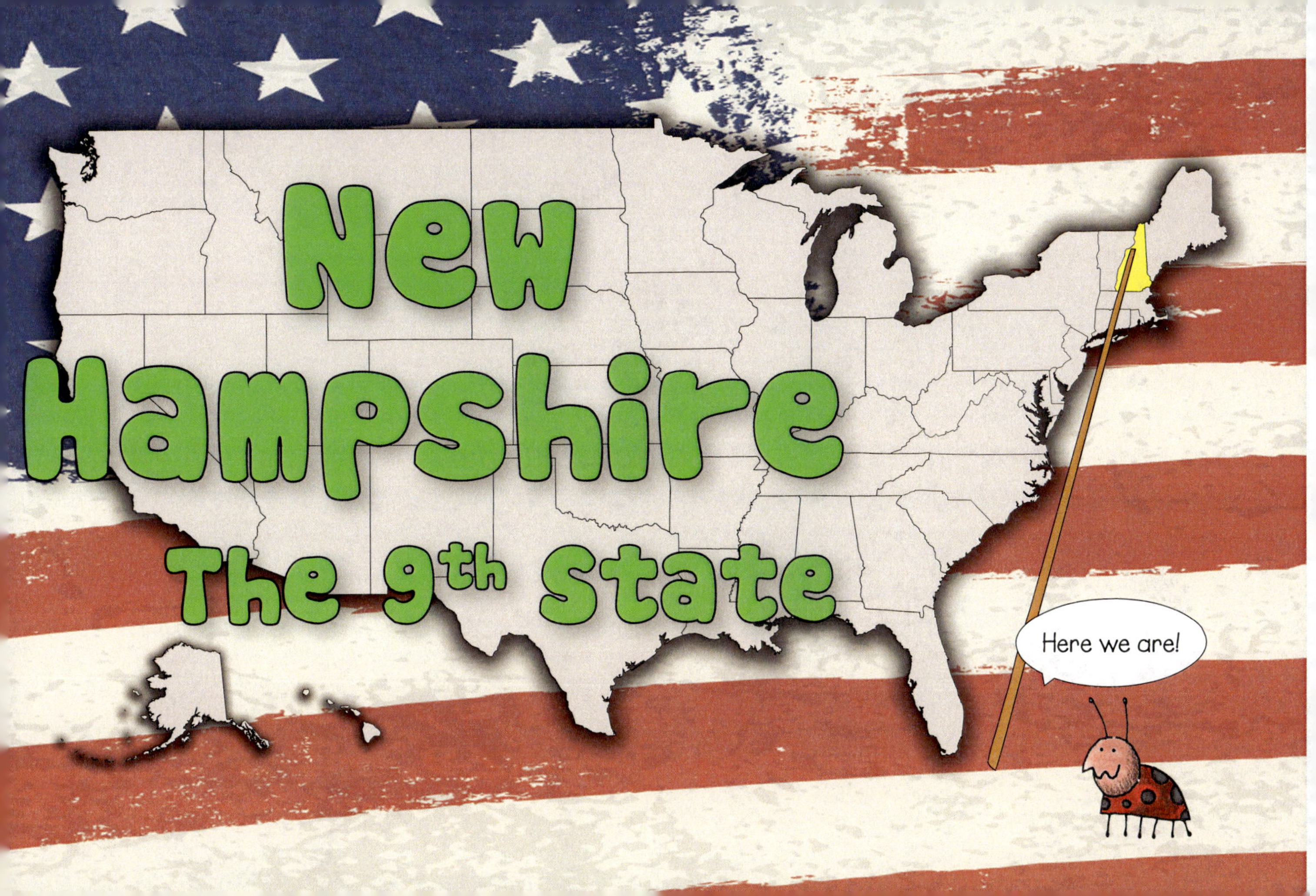

FLAG

I am the state flag.
I was adopted in 1909.

What color am I?
I am blue.

Look at me.
What else do you see?

I fly high over the state of New Hampshire!

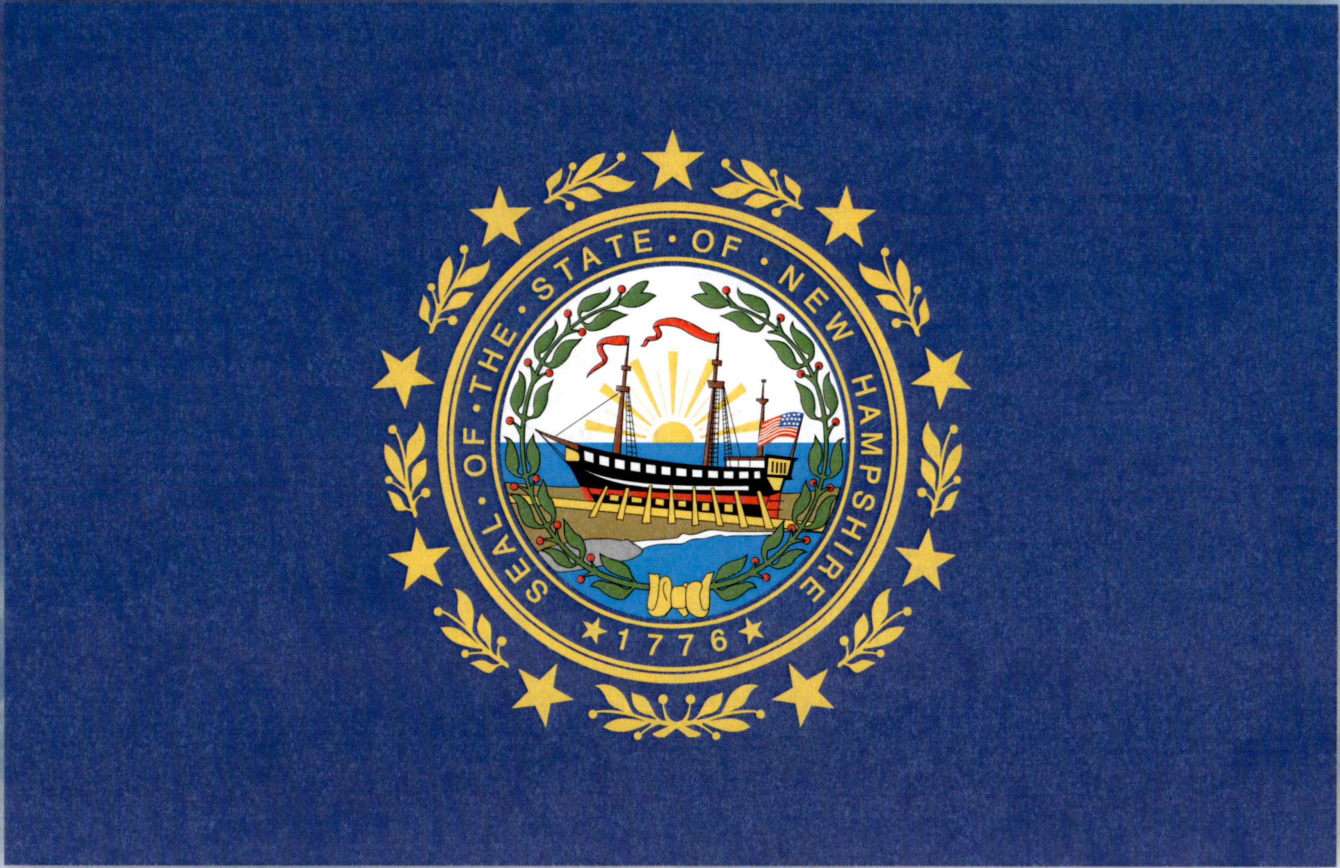
SEAL · OF · THE · STATE · OF · NEW HAMPSHIRE
1776

CAPITAL

Say hello to Concord,
the capital city of New Hampshire!

There is an important building in Concord.
It is the State House.
New Hampshire's laws are made there!

State House
Concord
Capital
DANIEL WEBSTER

SEAL

I am a seal,
but I am not the State Seal.
If I were, I would be very important.
I would be stamped on many official papers.
(Ouch, that might hurt!)

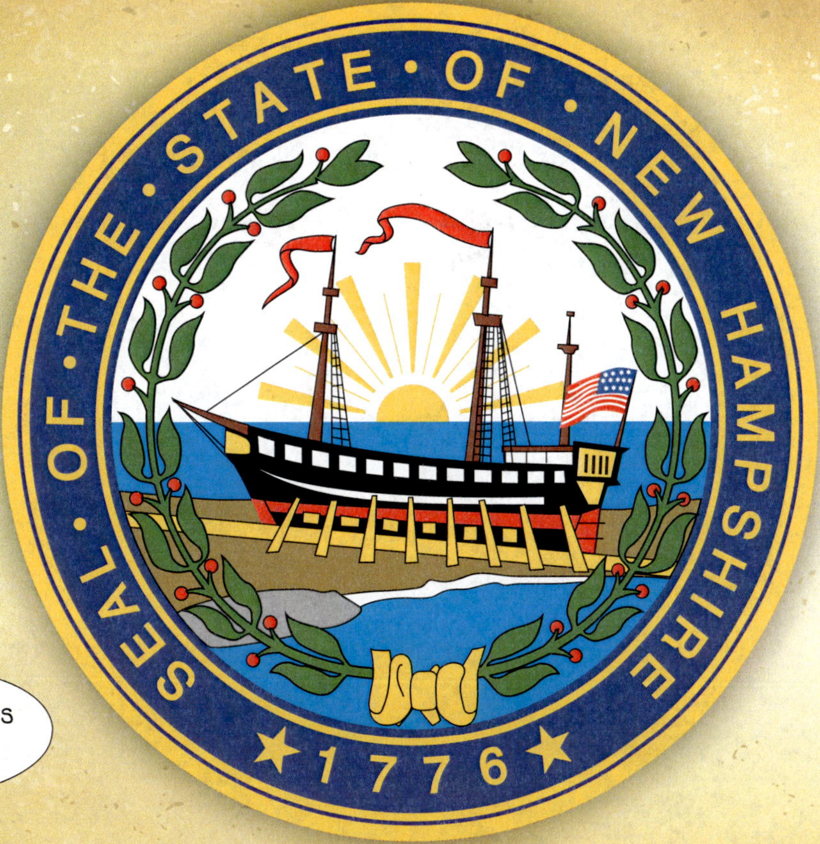
SEAL · OF · THE · STATE · OF · NEW HAMPSHIRE
1776

Now, that's official!

NICKNAME

State nicknames are fun!
State nicknames are great!
They share fun facts
about each state!

New Hampshire's nickname is "The Granite State."

New Hampshire has lots of granite!
Granite is often used to construct buildings.

The Granite State

BORDERS

Look at New Hampshire.
New Hampshire is in a region called "the Northeast."

New Hampshire borders three other states.
It also borders the country of Canada.
Find New Hampshire and its neighbors on the map!

Borders

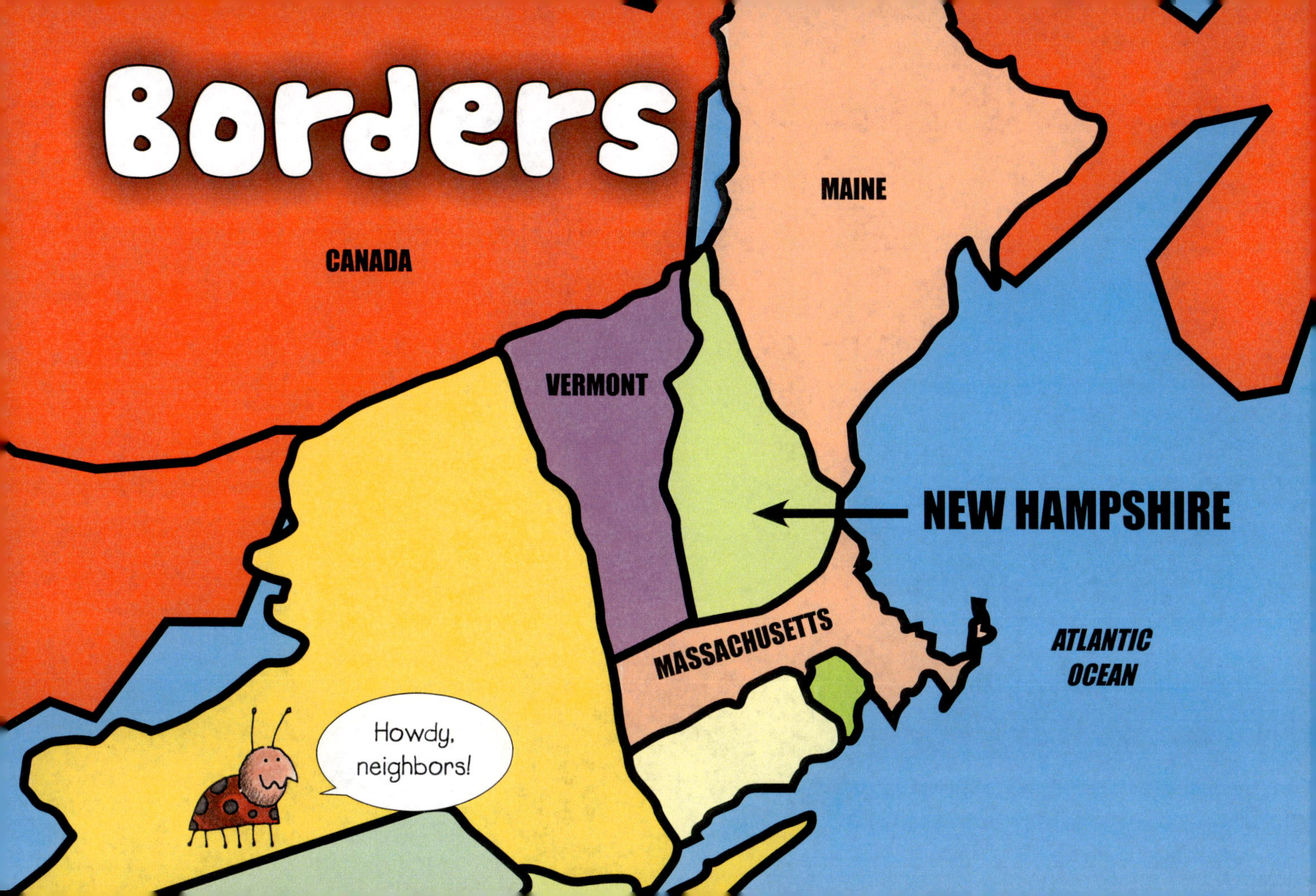

CANADA
MAINE
VERMONT
NEW HAMPSHIRE
MASSACHUSETTS
ATLANTIC OCEAN
Howdy, neighbors!

PRESIDENT

Franklin Pierce was the 14th President
of the United States of America.
He was born in New Hampshire!

Franklin Pierce was born in a log cabin in Hillsborough.
He was one of eight children.
His father fought in the American Revolution.

Franklin Pierce

PEOPLE

Many famous people

Josiah Bartlett

Signer of the Declaration of Independence

Sarah Josepha Hale

Author who wrote *Mary Had a Little Lamb*

Robert Frost

Poet who won four Pulitzer Prizes

call our state home!

Let's hang out!

Earl Tupper

Inventor of Tupperware plastic food storage containers

Alan Shepard

First American to travel in space

Jeanne Shaheen

First female governor of New Hampshire

PEOPLE

Purple Finch

I am the state bird, and I fly
over New Hampshire, proud and high.

As I fly, up in the sky,
I flap my wings to tell you "Hi!"

The New Hampshire state bird is the Purple Finch.

BIRD

Purple Lilac

FLOWER

I am the Purple Lilac.
I am the state flower.

I grow where it's warm and sunny.
I bloom in spring and summer.
I help make New Hampshire beautiful!

Look at me! Smell me!
I am known for my lovely fragrance!

White Birch

TREE

I am a White Birch—I'm the state tree.
All over New Hampshire is where to find me.

My roots run deep, they keep me strong.
I can live for hundreds of years—that's very long!

I stand up straight, big and tall.
Don't climb too high—it would hurt to fall!

Ladybug

INSECT

I am the Ladybug
I am the state insect.

I am a type of beetle.
I am red with black polka dots!

Gardeners and farmers love me.
I eat bugs off their plants.
I help New Hampshire crops grow.

Atlantic Ocean

Let's go to the beach!

We can swim in the waves.
We can play in the sand.

We can build a big castle
where water meets land.

New Hampshire's beaches are home to many animals:

Sea Turtles **Fish** **Birds** **Crabs** **Dolphins** **and More!**

BEACHES

White Mountains

MOUNTAINS

New Hampshire's White Mountains
are the place to be.
Hiking, fishing, camping—
fun for you and me.

Winter weather brings lots of snow.
Temperatures drop to freezing and below!

Rivers

RIVERS

New Hampshire has many rivers.
People like to use rivers for boating and fishing!

This habitat is home to many animals:

Birds Deer Snakes Frogs Fish and More!

New Hampshire is sometimes called the "Mother of Rivers." That's because five New England rivers start in New Hampshire!

Portsmouth Harbor Light

The Portsmouth Harbor Light is a lighthouse.
It stands in Portsmouth Harbor.
The original lighthouse tower was built in 1771.
Its job was to light the way for ships entering the harbor!

The Portsmouth Harbor Light is the only lighthouse on the mainland of New Hampshire!

New Hampshire Crops

AGRICULTURE

New Hampshire has many farms.
Why?
Because New Hampshire has good soil
and a mild climate!

Some of the top crops grown in New Hampshire are:

Nursery Plants **Sweet Corn** **Apples** **Potatoes**

Hey!
Don't forget about me!
I am a New Hampshire cow.
I produce lots of milk to make
dairy products!
Moooooooo!

Sports in New Hampshire

SPORTS

Baseball! Basketball! Football! Hockey!
New Hampshire has it all.

Whether you like to watch or play,
You are sure to have a ball!

Wildcats **Big Green** **Hawks**

Penmen

Ravens

& More!

New Hampshire: Home of Fall Foliage

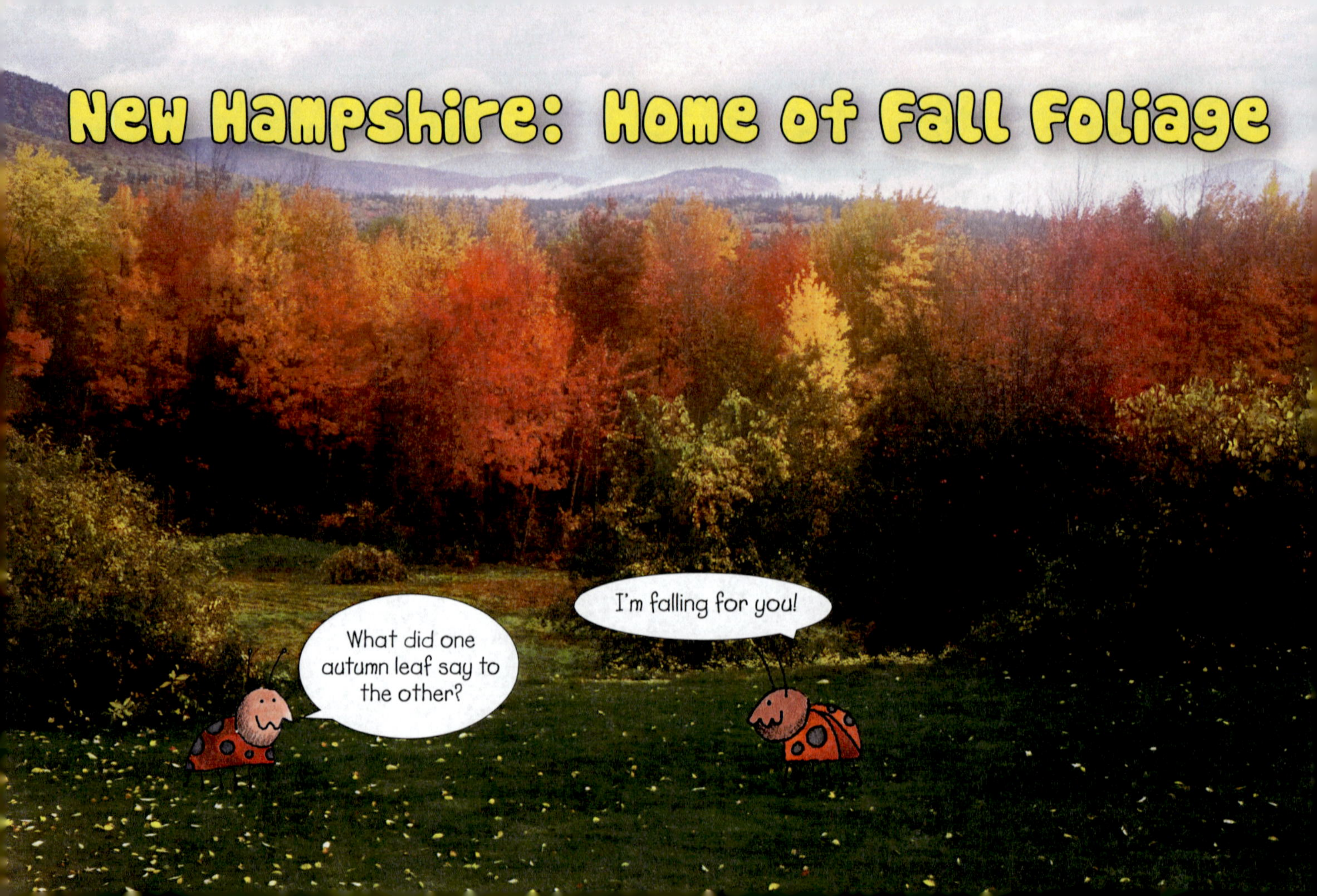

New Hampshire is known for its fantastic fall foliage!
Many people visit the state to see the
leaves changing color.
Visitors can look online for weekly updates
to learn where the best colors can be found!

The leaves on hardwood trees
turn to brilliant shades of gold,
orange, and red!

CLAIM TO FAME

GLOSSARY

climate: weather conditions in an area over a long period of time

colony: a settlement ruled by another country

elect: to choose someone by voting

foliage: leafy parts of a tree or plant

fragrance: a pleasant, sweet smell

habitat: a place where plants or animals naturally live

laws: rules made by the government

mainland: the main land mass of an area, as opposed to islands

original: first; earliest

region: an area that has similar characteristics